DJ MY WAY

A Journey of Music, Resilience, and Personal Transformation

AN AUTOBIOGRAPHY AND A GUIDE TO AWESOME CELEBRATIONS

RICK LOVE

© Copyright 2025

All rights reserved.

No part of this book may be used or reproduced mechanically, including photocopying, recording, taping, or any information storage retrieval system without the written permission of the publisher except in the case of brief quotations embodied in critical articles and reviews.

ISBN: 979-8-9933386-1-3 (hardcover)
979-8-9933386-0-6 (paperback)

Published by
My PreciousApple Publishing LLC

INTRODUCTION

I send my sincere thanks to my near and distant family members and friends, the readers of this book, whom I hope are many, and the almighty power above that inspired me to write this memoir of my experiences being and becoming a disc jockey. Everyone is special to me, and I realized I am blessed beyond measure to have my health and right mind (at times) to sit and write this book. Again, thank you for giving this book a chance to inform, educate, enlighten, and entertain you. Well enough with this small talk, and let me, as they say, "Get this party started…"

Rick Love
Thursday, August 06, 2020

TABLE OF CONTENTS

	Introduction	iii
Chapter One	How I Got Started	1
Chapter Two	Elementary School Times	5
Chapter Three	Under the Streetlights	9
Chapter Four	Moving To a New Neighborhood	15
Chapter Five	The Early Parties	19
Chapter Six	Tragedy	23
Chapter Seven	The Motown Review and My Friends	27
Chapter Eight	The Bad Times	31
Chapter Nine	Who Encouraged Me to Become a Disc Jockey (DJ)?	37
Chapter Ten	Music Lessons	43
Chapter Eleven	Growing Up Fast	45
Chapter Twelve	Booking a Gig	55
Chapter Thirteen	The Ideal Setup	57
Chapter Fourteen	The Crowds	59
Chapter Fifteen	Give Credit At All Times	63
Chapter Sixteen	The Microphone	65
Chapter Seventeen	Situational Music	69

Chapter Eighteen	The DJ Always Takes The Blame	71
Chapter Nineteen	The Strangest Things Happened	75
Chapter Twenty	The Bill Collector	83
Chapter Twenty-One	I Must Be Getting Old	87
Chapter Twenty-Two	Bring Back The Days	93
Chapter Twenty-Three	What You Will Need as a DJ	95
Chapter Twenty-Four	The Conclusion	97

The Poems

The Street Lights	11
The Motown Sound	29
Why Drugs?	33
They Stole My Car	40
I Just Don't Have It	52
The Microphone	67
Daddy, Please Spend Some Time With Me	80
Fees	85
They Broke into My Car	89
Guns	91

CHAPTER ONE

HOW I GOT STARTED

That question took me the longest to contemplate, but it started when I was five years old and even before then when my brother Lewis played in a band called "The 4 El Morocco's." He and his friends always practiced in my parents' living room, and I would watch them practice for as long as I was allowed to stay up at night to watch and listen to them.

Other than the drummer, they would set up in a few minutes, and my brother would play the lead guitar. I watched the bongo player tap out the beats that the entire band, including the drummer, would follow. That is when I began tapping my feet and trying to snap my fingers. I found myself getting up and dancing, and my brother kept reminding me that I was not dancing to the beat. I didn't know what he was talking about until I watched him, and his fellow band members tap their feet while playing.

I want to say that tapping to the beat or finding the rhythm was inherited or easy, but it wasn't. I had to work on it for a few weeks and share my newfound activity with my friends.

We were all as happy as we thought we should be. Although we lived in the all-black neighborhood known as "Black Bottom," none of us were ever hungry because our parents worked and provided adequate meals for us. We seldom dined at each other's houses, but when we were outside playing, none of us were hungry, and we knew what time dinner was being served.

I thought I finally got the hang of clapping and stomping to the beat, and I tested it out almost daily because everyone knew someone in a band. The bands would play music in many of my friend's houses as they practiced for shows in nearby bars, nightclubs, dance halls, and restaurants. This was in the mid to late 1950s when the music business was a huge source of income for musicians and vendors of all kinds, including clothing stores, record shops, and pawn shops. It was a profitable business that many people, talented or otherwise, were anxious to get involved in.

Plus, this was a time before black people were allowed to live anywhere other than in their neighborhoods or, as they were called, a reservation or the ghetto. It was a time when musicians would load the back of a truck with an open flatbed and play music as they rode through the neighborhood, and everyone would come out to wave at them as they slowly passed by. My brother was a part of those bands, and as much as I wanted to ride along, he would never take me because he said it was too dangerous.

After being taught by one of the 4 El Morocco band members, I began popping my fingers, and that lesson remains in place today. Learning to snap my fingers and dance to the beat started it all; right after that, in 1957, my father gave me my first allowance. He told me that each week when I was good in school and I did my chores around the house, he would give me an allowance of one dollar. In the 1950s, that was a lot for a kid to receive because there were many five-and-dime stores, and a whole dollar went a long way for my sweet tooth and my friends.

That was a secondary concern because the first thing I did with my first dollar was go to the record store and buy a record. I bought "Shake Rattle and Roll" by Big Joe Turner and "Jim Dandy" by Lavern Baker. Those records came to a grand total of ninety-four cents, including the sales tax. I went home, used the family record player, and played both songs all day while snapping my fingers and trying to do the new dance craze, "The Hully Gully."

I decided that music and collecting records was my hobby, and that was the inspiration I needed to listen to music every day, find whatever I considered "the jam," and buy it at the music store with my money. I strayed from the record buying habit on many occasions and got into trouble most of the time when I purchased something else. I recall the corner stores were usually owned by black or white couples who lived either upstairs from their store or close by in the neighborhood.

They were the true definition of the "Ma and Pa" shops, and they knew all the kids and their parents. The stores were a place where we trusted the owners, and so did our parents. One day, when I spent my money on something other than records. I kept buying what the kids and I called "Wine Candy," and when our parents found out the name, we called it, it created quite a stir in the neighborhood. We were told not to buy it anymore for fear of it being a treat that contained alcohol, and the next thing we knew, the police stopped by the corner store to investigate what was being sold.

As it turned out, it was what we know today as "Jolly Ranchers" and "Orange Slices," and the manufacturer immediately changed the names for obvious reasons. Right after that, I returned to my buying music habits, and my record holder was beginning to fill up with those brittle and often scratchy 78s. They didn't last long before getting brittle and breaking very easily. That meant if you liked that record and played it all the time, you had to buy it again and again. That was one of the best benefits of the music industry, and that was selling more and more records. It was not unusual for everyone, including adults, to have a record collection, and that was another reason that inspired me to listen to and collect music as a prestigious sign of being in the know and popular because I had most if not all the so-called jams in my collection.

CHAPTER TWO

ELEMENTARY SCHOOL TIMES

I was in kindergarten when I sang songs I heard on the radio, and the kids in my class would sing along. I was the one who started singing songs, and of course, one song got me into trouble. I started singing "Little Sally Walker sitting in a saucer. Ride Sally, ride, wipe your weeping eyes. Put your hands on your hips and let your backbone slip. Aww, shake to the east. Aww, shake it to the west. Aww, shake to the one that you love best." That became a major problem that got me kicked out of school for a few days. I avoided a butt-whooping because I told my parents I was kicked out for singing a song. That was a saving grace, and when mom gave a butt whooping, it was short and almost painless. But a whooping given by my dad was short and painful, and the welts from his belt lasted a few days.

Those were the times when me or a classmate would come to school with welts on our arms and legs, and it was an accepted occurrence that you got an ass whooping, and it was no big deal. Nowadays, it would bring the criminal justice system to your home, and child abuse charges would be levied against parents. It is a documented fact that the American generation that has earned the highest level of education in American history is the Baby Boomer Generation (1946 to 1964). That is what happened when parents were allowed to be parents, and the money they earned for the corporations that employed them was given to the workers and not diverted elsewhere, which is common today. The stock market, Wall Street, and Silicon Valley were not nearly as influential, or greed driven as they are nowadays.

I mentioned that because our parents had enough money to take care of a middle-class home in a nice neighborhood, where they could raise their children with the resources needed to provide them the chance for a quality education. That included music, dancing, and singing lessons. That also included having the money to send their children to school with clean clothes and stomachs full of food, along with lunch money or a lunch box. Those essential facts contributed to the musicians that emerged during that time and fed the music industry with talent that has not been matched since.

It bothers me to think about if Barry Gordy, The Temptations, Smokey Robinson, Norman Whitfield, Holland Dozier Holland, The Four Tops, Marvin Gaye, The Supremes, The Marvelettes, Hank Ballard, Bill Doggett, and Stevie Wonder were not exposed to music when they were in grade school, the world would've missed the creative art, music, and literature that will inspire future generations and last forever. I attribute my exposure to music to those experiences, and children in grade schools nowadays are often given police officer exposure instead of guidance counselors and music teachers. That is one of the most important things I've noticed about the difference between new and old-school times. They found a way to make people happy while studying music, and that is why I made it my life's goal to know and play the music I love for myself and others.

The nursery rhymes and the songs children learn in school, including America the Beautiful, The National Anthem, and the ABCs, are all results of music being used as tools of learning and enjoyment...

CHAPTER THREE

UNDER THE STREETLIGHTS

As a child raised on Detroit's East Side in the late 1950s and early 1960s, I was blessed with being required to be in the house or within calling distance when the streetlights came on. It was a year-round unwritten law. If I was not near or in my house when the streetlights came on, I sure as hell didn't do that again. The Streetlights were our version of a cellphone or pager, and the unwritten law was universal in my neighborhood, and no one dared to cross that line. However, when the streetlights came on and the children were securely in their homes, the spring, summer, and fall air would be filled with the sounds of many groups of teenagers and a few men and women over and under the age of 21 as they would meet under the streetlights and sing acapella.

They would harmonize and sing like nothing anyone had ever heard before. The songs they sang were mainly popular radio hits during that time. I remember hearing "Sincerely" and "Life is But a Dream" by the Harptones. "So Much in Love" by the Tymes, "Farewell My Love" by The Temptations, and one of my favorites, "In The Still of The Night" by the Five Satins. On occasions during the Christmas Holidays, they would also invite their parents and neighbors to sing Christmas Carols from door to door and sing Christmas songs by Nat King Cole, The Platters, and the Drifters. My family and I, along with many of our neighbors, would sit on our porches and listen to those golden voices fill the air with the sweet sounds of street corner harmony. It is so sad that video cameras and smartphones were not available to record the wonderful sounds of their singing voices.

I think it was a folk tale, but a few of those groups that sang on the street corners in Detroit and around the USA were discovered by record producers and awarded recording contracts. Groups like The Persuasions, The Originals, the Dramatics, the Esquires, The Primes (The Temptations), and Stevie Wonder are where many of them were discovered because of their street corner performances. At that time, music was a profitable business because you had to buy a record to get it, and record companies knew that if they released good music, they would sell thousands of copies every day. There were record stores in almost every block, and they were also located inside local grocery stores and gift shops. Modern-day downloading and copying inhibit that scenario nowadays, and all that is left is being able to form singing groups for fun and not always for financial gains.

I wrote this poem for those moments that I so clearly remember:

The Street Lights
by Rick Love
Tuesday, September 01, 2009

A silent flicker on a pole with lights of blue or gold,

You knew what time it was, as you were told.

As time has passed and things got better,

The common threads of hope pulled us all together.

The streetlights would flicker on most city streets.

The children would run home like they had hot seats!

It was not the fear of the moonlight that glowed on their cheeks.

It was the wrath of their parents for staying in the streets!

The streetlights were a tool of discipline and control.

It was totally understood by the young and the old.

A muted silence and a hush fell upon a crowd,

It was the unspoken words that were thought of out loud.

"Is your child outside and the streetlights are on?

It's almost dark now, and your child should be at home."

Every adult was respected, meddlesome, and courteous.

It was not child abuse. This was "community service!"

If you were not in the house when the streetlights came on,

You were punished by the adults who were inside your home.

This old-school way punished us for not obeying this law!

It was an unwritten rule, and you were always on call.

It was these unwritten laws that protected the big and small.

Disobey them and you could not go out at all.

The old school ways worked, and they worked quite well.

Does society make them too difficult to tell?

I believe this worked and it will work again.

Let's rally our neighbors and treat them as friends.

There will be difficult things for our children to understand.

They might disagree before they follow our commands.

I will join in as a parent and as a friend.

Just tell me your child's name, and then we can begin.

The old-school laws could truly work out.

Bottom line says our children should be safe in the house.

This unwritten law of common sense is where it begins.

Children are in the house when the daylight ends…this is too simple…

Maybe one day, a group of talented young men and women will stand under the streetlight in front of or near my house and sing that old-school harmony so I can enjoy them again along with my neighbors. Those were great memories, and I often remind myself that being inspired by good music makes me think of the money it made for too few people who sang those wonderful songs. Those songs and those times are priceless, and I hope those joys of history will repeat soon.

CHAPTER FOUR

MOVING TO A NEW NEIGHBORHOOD

Living in a black neighborhood when a doctor lived next door to a factory worker, a garbage man lived next to a postal worker, or a lawyer lived next to a party store owner was not unusual. The local stores were owned by people living in the community, and many people who frequented our neighborhood were public servants and local celebrities who wore uniforms. The Detroit Tigers Major League Baseball team had many players as residents in the neighborhoods, and they would sign autographs for the kids and sponsor summer camps to teach them how to play baseball. This was before the Civil Rights Voting Act, the law that was supposed to stop the redlining of black people to keep them from living wherever their money could carry them.

That change in policy allowed my parents to move to a primarily white neighborhood in Northwest Detroit, where I was one of only six black students enrolled in the local elementary school. I was the class clown in the school because the things we were taught were easy for me to understand, but the first two days in the new school proved to be extremely difficult.

The curriculum, a few hazing incidents, and being called names like 8 Ball, Tar Baby, and Little Richard (one of my childhood music heroes) made things difficult. I was not used to standing up in class and reciting the capital cities of the United States. I didn't know the difference between Christianity and Judaism. I had never experienced those challenges, and having a television in the school room where I learned Spanish and French and enjoyed hot lunches with several flavors of milk were things I had never experienced.

Suddenly, my place as one of the most popular kids in the school was replaced by feeling lost and out of touch with new academic challenges. I think my experience was felt by the other few black students in my school, and it was noticed by one of the black teachers who passed away several years ago, Mrs. Catherine Blackwell. She understood what we were going through, and she sent a letter home to each of the black children's parents asking if we could stay at school for an extra hour each day so she could tutor us on her own time at no charge and bring us up to the same level as the white students. Plus, she took all of us home in her car afterward.

All of our parents agreed, and I can honestly say that Mrs. Blackwell is partly responsible for the person I am today. She was truly an unsung hero in the Detroit Public School System who helped countless lucky children become responsible adults. I give her and, of course, my parents credit for inspiring me to listen to the advice of my elders and to stay focused on what I wanted to do, and to me, it was listening to all kinds of music and owning a record collection.

I did try to lead the class in the new school in song, but I soon found out that the songs I knew were unfamiliar to my white classmates. I began listening to the sounds of British groups and watching American Bandstand, Shindig, and Hullabaloo on prime-time television. I tried again to lead the classes in song, and I was ignored until I began singing songs by The Beatles, The Monkees, The Dave Clark Five, Bobby Goldsboro, The Four Seasons, The Beach Boys, Shirley Ellis, and The Rolling Stones. I then captured their attention, which resulted in finding the key to playing to and pleasing the audience in front of me.

I occasionally sang a Motown song, and they also caught on to singing those songs. This is a time when the music industry was riding high, and thousands of record stores and live concerts were never-ending, and all were quite profitable. Yes, knowing all kinds of music was what I envisioned as a key to my growth and a way to socialize with anyone because it is a common path that most of the kids I grew up with wanted to walk down together.

CHAPTER FIVE

THE EARLY PARTIES

I've always tried to have a good record collection. I've always enjoyed using electronic gadgets, and I operated movie projectors in school. I also used my small record player for class projects, which is one of my favorite things to do. Those were my first experiences of playing music to a crowd, and I was always asked to bring my records to someone's house, as they called an impromptu party to celebrate just being alive as the reason. That quickly evolved into being invited to attend birthday parties, and I was always asked to dance and play my music for the crowd.

I even got a few invitations to my white classmates' parties. I became popular because of my record collection and my willingness to show them the newest dances and, jokingly, at times, teach them the simple art of rhythm. I would start by simply asking everyone to snap their fingers. To my disbelief, many of them didn't know how to snap their fingers, and after showing them a few times, they caught on. These simple things that made people happy have also given me great memories that have lasted since then.

My best childhood memory is that while attending a birthday party for a special friend (I would write her name, but to keep her name private), I will call her Remy. Remy had a 12th or 13th birthday party, and it was three years after we moved into the neighborhood, and almost half of the white families had moved out. However, the few remaining white families were our friends, and we had a great time at Remy's party. That was the first time I played Musical Chairs and Spin the Bottle. Both games required music, and I was asked to work the record player. I was all set for musical chairs and asked not to be left out of the Spin the Bottle game simply because I wanted to kiss the girls...

Yes, that was important to a young man in his early teens, and this was no different. That is when I figured out that putting on a record that played for longer than the usual three to five minutes made the difference. At that time, 33-1/2 RPM vinyl records were available, but they cost more than the 45s, and they usually consisted of a collection of songs first released as singles. The albums had liner notes on the cover and pictures, and they often included articles about the artists and a copy of the song lyrics.

The 33-1/2 albums were often covered in plastic shrink wrap to assure the buyer they were new, and many times, you left the shrink wrap on it as a symbol of just adding it to your music collection. However, if it sat on the floor or the shelf too long, the plastic on the outside would shrink and cause the record inside to warp or get out of round. That was an ongoing problem with plastic records and something we dealt with until the cassette tapes were introduced in the mid-1960s. They were a direct spin-off of the reel-to-reel tapes, and several manufacturers decided to make cassette tapes with smaller players to tap into the record-selling marketplace.

I had limited experience using cassette tapes to spin music for an audience. Companies like Zenith, Teac, Panasonic, Magnavox, Sony, RCA Victor, and AIWA manufactured the players, and a few had a slight problem with hissing. The hissing was fixable, but it placed the players that eliminated the hissing sounds out of the price range for most buyers. Most of the music was good, and the blank cassette tapes were what I considered the beginning of the end for music being copied from the radio and many other sources.

CHAPTER SIX

TRAGEDY

It was a bright Saturday morning on June 03, 1967, when my family ventured out to Sears and Roebuck to purchase a few items for doing yard work. We picked up a rake, a push (not power) lawnmower, and other garden tools. On the way home, my sister Kathy and I asked if we could stop by the Dairy Queen to get some ice cream treats. It was located on Mc Nichols and Livernois in Detroit. My dad was driving our 1964 4-door Ford Galaxy 500, and we pulled into the DQ parking lot. My mother and sister got out of the car to go to the window to order our treats, and my dad and I sat in the car. My sister bought my favorite ice cream, a banana split in a cup to me, and she gave my dad his favorite treat, an orange sherbet push cup, and she returned to the front of the building to get her ice cream.

I was looking out the back seat passenger window at the DQ counter, and I heard my dad breathing hard and gasping for air. I saw him slump over in the seat, and I knew something was wrong, and I called out his name. "Daddy, Daddy, what's wrong? What's wrong?" He didn't respond, and I leaned forward, and he was sweating but also icy cold. Not thinking about anything else, I poured some of my ice cream onto his chest as a way I thought to revive him. When he didn't respond, I dropped my ice cream, exited the car, and ran franticly to the DQ counter. I told my mom that something was wrong with Daddy. She ran back to the car, and the DQ owner came out the back door, saw my dad slumped over, went inside, and called the police for help.

The police and an ambulance arrived in about 10 minutes, and they had to ask us to step back so they could examine him. They decided it would be best to put him on a stretcher and take him to the hospital. Then, out of the blue and without provocation, a white fireman asked my mom in a nasty tone of voice, "Has he been drinking?"... I saw it in her eyes that she was hurt when that question was asked, and she politely told him that he hadn't been drinking. That question still bothers me today because it was only a little after noon, and a question like that was probably legitimate, but it was presented the wrong way in an impolite, racist-sounding tone of voice.

They loaded my dad into the ambulance and took him to Sinai Hospital. My mother called her sister (my Aunt Mary), and she came and took us to the hospital. While we were on the way to the hospital, she turned on the radio, and the song "Ain't No Mountain High Enough" came on. Every time I hear that song, I think about that day, and I've made myself smile.

My mom, my sister, and I arrived at the hospital and went to the emergency room and asked for our dad. They said he was in one of the emergency holding rooms, and we were directed to where he was.

We found his room, and we were relieved to see him lying there with many tubes and cables attached to him, hoping that he would be alright. As a 14-year-old and my sister a nine-year-old, we had no idea what to expect. This was the first time we experienced a trauma that happened to one of our parents. My dad was talking to us with an oxygen tube in his nose as he tried to reposition the monitor patches on his legs.

We spoke to him for a few minutes, and all of a sudden, his eyes rolled back in his head, and he pulled the tube out of his nose, and we all screamed for the doctors and nurses to come back right away. They huddled around him as we stepped out of the room, and they worked on him frantically. We were asked to wait in the lounge down the hall, and the doctors came in and told us "his heart stopped beating," and they were working on him, and he would update us of any changes. The doctor came out several more times, and after the fourth time to talk to us, we were told, "he was gone!"

My mother, my sister, and I all screamed and cried really loud. About 20 minutes later, a nice lady not wearing a hospital gown asked my mom if she could take my sister and me to another room while she handled the paperwork regarding my dad. She agreed, and this young black woman, who I believed was in her thirties, talked to us and calmed us down. To this day, I think she was a psychologist who specialized in children. She managed to calm us down and made it easier to accept what just happened.

My older brother arrived at the hospital when my sister and I were in the parking lot, taking my dad's belongings to the car. I cried and told him that our dad was gone, and he ran into the hospital to be with our mom. We finally left the hospital and arrived home, and my mom told a neighbor who lived across the street that my dad just passed away. The following day, we woke up to the neighbors in front of our house cutting and edging our grass and trimming the bushes in our front and back yards. That is one of my fondest memories of our neighbors being nice to me and my family in our time of need. Plus, from that day on, I learned to appreciate my neighbors, and being a good neighbor has guided my efforts toward everyone I am blessed to live near in my neighborhood.

CHAPTER SEVEN

THE MOTOWN REVIEW AND MY FRIENDS

It was the mid to late 1960s, and Motown was inspiring America and the world with music and lyrics that were outstanding, creative, and never will be forgotten. The children in our schools always looked up to the Motown stars as community leaders and someone we wanted to be. We would have Motown spottings when the stars would be seen riding around the neighborhood in luxury convertible cars, wearing fine clothes, and waving at us as they passed by. They were our heroes, and to be like them with fame and fortune was just about every young man and woman's dream in my neighborhood.

I remember when Duke Fakir of the Four Tops went into the drug store around the corner from my house on Seven Mile and a few of my friends and I saw him go inside. We immediately formed a line outside the store and started singing "Still Waters" as best we could, and when he walked out, we smiled at him and kept on singing. He looked at us and politely said, "Just keep practicing fellas, just keep practicing," which made our day. The Motown family was considered part of our community, and we embraced Motown as a "Wonder of the World" located in Detroit.

I made it a point to buy every record they released, knowing that the different labels they used were an easy reminder of how well-organized they were. Most people like me would dance and try to make dance routines like the Motown stars we watched at their shows and on television. Many of their dance moves were copied and performed at just about every talent show I attended and entered, which is true today. The acts that inspired youth to perform were most notably James Brown, The Temptations, The Four Tops, The Supremes, The Marvelettes, Jackie Wilson, The Dramatics, The Manhattans, and in the 1970s and 80s, and to this day, the Jackson 5 with Michael Jackson, Prince, and The Sugar Hill Gang.

It was a great time to be proud of being a young man inspired by music. Those days will forever remain in my daily thinking and are one of the reasons why the Motown sound will never get old, especially when it's being played for my ears to hear. I mentioned the Motown sound because it was instrumental in my decision to love music and inspired many musicians and songwriters to pursue a career in music. I enrolled in the Motown Writers Guild, and unfortunately, none of my songs were ever used to produce a song. That shortfall inspired me to write:

The Motown Sound
by Rick Love

There was Smokey, Otis, Paul, Melvin, David, and Eddie.

They were also backed by the Funk Brothers and managed by Shelly.

They sang soulful sounds that we hummed along to.

The Marvelettes and The Four Tops also sang as their voices came shining through.

We were all so excited when their songs were played...

The Motown Revue displayed their talents during the Christmas holidays.

It was the event of the year and Little Stevie Wonder turned the place out.

He played the harmonica and made everybody shout.

The Supremes were beautiful, and The Miracles were cool.

They often inspired the community dress code rules.

It was a great time when everyone dressed so fine.

And James Brown came to town all the time.

He announced on the radio that he would be the sharpest person there.

He would come out on stage and aahs would be heard everywhere.

The Christmas Holidays are never the same.

The Motown Review highlighted Detroit's Hall of Fame.

It would be nice if it came back to Detroit again.

It would be another delightful way to enjoy inspirational sounds.

As we welcome the new generations to the beauty of Motown.

CHAPTER EIGHT

THE BAD TIMES

I was in the choir in high school, singing first and second tenor, and I thought I was doing well. Then, one day, and to my surprise, I was asked to sing a note or two. The teacher informed me that my voice had changed, and rather than place me in the baritone section or elsewhere, I was sent to study hall. I don't think that teacher knew how devastated I was to be excused from the music class, and to this day, I strongly believe that it was my antics and outgoing silliness that she disliked and not my singing voice. So, I sat in study hall, disappointed, hurt, and embarrassed because I had been removed from the choir.

I was hurt, and I began thinking that getting high from drinking or smoking weed was a way to ease my disappointment. Then, I began thinking that getting high was the best way to get excited about the music I listened to and wanted to play to an audience. I listened to the music of the number one-rated guitarist in the 20th century, Jimi Hendrix. He was credited for inventing Psychedelic Music. That also inspired me not to think of drugs or alcohol use as another way to enjoy music. It was a mistake, and my personal saying to everyone who thinks so is "WEED = Will Erase Every Dream," and it was said that nothing will happen to you if you smoke it. They were right. As a young person, nothing will happen to you because you will be content to do absolutely nothing. You won't go out and party. You won't care about getting dressed up, and you become short-tempered and difficult to get along with.

I write this not from what I've read but from what I've experienced, and I've witnessed many of my friends act and fail the same way I did. So, getting high and trying to entertain are losing propositions, and many artists who were said to use drugs and alcohol either died early or spent time in the criminal justice system. Drugs have certainly ruined many lives, and the examples of great entertainers using drugs as a way to please their followers was a culture built on deceit and caused irreparable harm to more people than can be counted.

You might ask yourself, "Why Drugs?" The following poem was written during one of my moments of frustration.

Why Drugs?
by Rick Love
Thursday, March 26, 2009

Drugs have been around since the beginning of time.

They were made accidentally, and they were really hard to find.

Alcohol appeared when the farmers used the waste from their crops.

The Indians used berries, herbs, and spices to make their pain stop.

The ancient Egyptians used oils and clay to end their day.

They took venom from animals to heal, sacrifice, and pray.

The Inca Tribe wanted pain and relief.

They planted, cooked, and processed the sun baked coca leaves.

The ancient scientists used alcohol as a healing blood thinner.

They soon mixed it with sugar, honey, corn, and vinegar.

The phrase alcoholic was introduced to the English language

It consisted of beer, wine, and hard liquor in a world of anguish.

They caused belly aches, kidney stones, and acute liver damage.

They had problems with addictions as something they could not manage.

The poppy seed was thought of as a beautiful plant.

It grew and was harvested to soothe and heal with its magical trance.

Opium, morphine, and heroin were soon discovered.

It ruined the new world that has yet to recover.

They gave it to the chemist and made illegal treats.

They put it into hospitals as a way to keep it off the streets.

They asked what to do with this powder we waste?

They created heroin to make users want another taste.

They smoked it at first then they used a small straw.

They wanted more than just that and used a needle to blood draw.

Sharing of needles was practiced a bit too much.

A blood disease called Aids created quite a fuss.

Getting high with a needle began to stop as sickness was on track.

The chemist got the idea that smoking drugs had to make a comeback.

Then they introduced smoke-able cocaine known as crack.

Oh, what a rush it gave using it for the first time. You were set up for life with a future filled with crime.

This new phenomenon became an overwhelming problem

It upset the leaders of the world and dared them to solve them.

Hast made waste and allot of us paid.

We were made into modern day chemical slaves.

The rich got richer and even their kids gave it a try.

Money was not an object if they wanted to get high.

As long as the demand overcomes the human mind,

A product for sale might be worth buying.

A hit, a smoke, a drink will last until the ends of all time,

Demand for drugs will keep it going until the very end of mankind…

I would discourage anyone, no matter who they are, from using street drugs for whatever reason because it has been proven to be detrimental to their health and their progress toward their goals in life. As the Baretta song says, "Don't Do it...."

Many people object to what I've written because they have either acquired success or are stuck not being successful, and drugs are a way of making a bad situation seem better. Everything from advertising alcohol and cigarettes on television to a culture of bad behavior and incarceration is meant to happen. The historical so-called "War on Drugs" has been nothing but disastrous in the black and brown communities.

Here again the question you are asking yourself: "What does this have to do with spinning music for a crowd?" When you have to rely on something other than your natural ability to entertain, you stand a good chance of losing the ability or desire to make other people happy. Entertaining will eventually get in the way of your drug or alcohol use, and that is self-explanatory.

CHAPTER NINE

WHO ENCOURAGED ME TO BECOME A DISC JOCKEY (DJ)?

After being fortunate enough to live through using drugs and alcohol and not get hooked or addicted, I finally straightened up. I got a good paying job in the factory. It was hard work, and because of my soft drug use, being hardheaded, and not listening to some of my elder's good advice, I was headed in the wrong direction. My deflection from progressing toward a successful future was doubtful and I was a soft drug user when I was given an apron, a hammer, and a screwdriver and placed on an automotive assembly line.

I also had a great job before being sent to the factory, but I blew it because of my oversleeping and my lack of a sense of urgency to get to work on time. Yes, I was fired for being late, but my work was good. My work performance was the only reason I was told to get an attendance record at another job and that my returned application would be considered for employment. With that being said, that is how I ended up on the assembly line for two years before returning to the job that fired me for tardiness. I spent 36-1/2 years on that first job before I was forced to retire.

At any rate, I was back to my old ways, singing songs while working hard on the assembly line, and on occasions, my coworkers would join in. This was in the early 1970s when Motown and countless record companies across America were producing hit records, and I continued to buy them. I used at least fifty dollars a week buying 33-1/2 albums and 45s to add to my record collection. Plus, I purchased a car and a lot of fashionable clothes, and I went to just about every concert that came to Detroit, oftentimes taking a different girleach time.

I purchased a used 1969 Ford Shelby GT 500, and I ended up spending a lot of money fixing it up, only to have it stolen from the parking lot while I was at work. Instead of listening to my elders, I once again acted irresponsibly as I was working for the car and not letting the car work for me. I guess God had other plans for me, and He took the car away. I bought a used 1971 Dodge Charger to go back and forth to work, and once again, my record collection and going to concerts became my focus.

I wrote this because having a car you worked so hard fixing could never be replaced by a few dollars as compensation from an insurance company. This poem was written because of my car being stolen, and I included it because the painful memories remain in my mind.

They Stole My Car
by Rick Love

I went to work one morning as early as could be.

I drove my 1969 Mustang Shelby GT.

I paid the parking attendant the money he needed.

I locked the car and removed some wires from it.

I was at work and never knew anything was wrong.

I talked to a so-called friend and he mentioned my car was gone.

I wondered how he knew that before me.

I went to the parking lot, and broken glass was there to see.

I went to the attendant angry as I could be.

I asked him if he saw them stealing from me.

He acted like he didn't understand

And it took every ounce of me to keep from hitting that man.

I was upset that a car I worked for was taken from me.

I never bothered anyone, and I would ride people for free.

Then it dawned on me that the friend I just spoke to knew.

He was probably a co-conspirator and got paid for what they wanted to do.

I never saw him again after that day.

I guess he knew my questions would be asked in a violent way.

It was a message from God to take it away.

That car was a distraction to my goals every day.

The insurance company paid me what they thought I deserved.

They could never compensate me for the memories it served.

I forgot about it in time, and I rode the bus every day.

I would feel sorry for myself to be used in that way.

I went back to my music, and my old job called me back.

I was settled in and motivated, and my spirit never cracked.

Life has many changes that are difficult sometimes.

We have to know the reason and enjoy great times.

Lessons are blessings, and trust is earned.

Always let it be told that fate helped us learn…

That poem strays a little off topic, but it was another way that my attention kept returning to music and away from the bad influences on my future.

CHAPTER TEN

MUSIC LESSONS

Before I decided to join the workforce in the late 1960s and early 1970s, I knew I was the next Jimi Hendrix. I could almost play a few of his hit songs on my guitar. It was typical for the kids in the neighborhood to form bands, and I was no different. It was me and my friends in the basement of whoever's house when our parents weren't at home and trying to play the songs we heard on the radio and in our music collections. I would play the lead guitar and the bongos, my best friend Stevie would play bass, and he was also our band's leader. I admit to not being as good as he was, but I owned the amplifiers, and it was my basement where we practiced without annoying our parents.

We were inseparable when it came to playing and practicing, and that day arrived when we played at an event. Yes, we were hired to play at a party, and I was as nervous as I could be. I was so nervous that I declined to play, and another friend who played the guitar better than I could was asked to fill in my spot. I remember pretending to be sick and unable to perform, and the guy who played the drums, Greg, asked his neighbor to come along and play with them.

After what I thought was a life-threatening moment, I decided it was time to get some professional music lessons. I went to a building on the corner of Kirby and Woodward in Detroit and signed up for guitar lessons. I paid my hard-earned $10 to enroll, and during the first lesson I took, I was asked to identify a music note on a scale, and I had absolutely no idea what it was. I later found it was the beginning of music, and it was a whole note of middle C. That was the last time I went to lessons there because I wanted to learn to play and not read music, which I later learned was so important.

Reading music is like learning a new language, which is the foundation of music, and finding what notes to play on a music sheet is important. As they say, I learned the hard way, and playing the guitar and dreams of being the next Jimi Hendrix were not to be.

CHAPTER ELEVEN

GROWING UP FAST

After working on the assembly line for a few long years, I learned that the world is much bigger than my problems and no one cares if I fail. Everyone seems to care when we succeed, and smoking weed and staying in my own little world got me nowhere, and changes were needed. The true road to recovery is admitting your problems and doing something about them soon. Well, at least it did in my situation.

I began to pay attention more and more to the local news, and I quit smoking cigarettes. That was the hardest thing I ever did up to that point in my life and I always had music playing on my radio and my music collection to fill in the social gaps I created when I was smoking reefers. Yes, that is the other name for Marijuana, and calling it weed or smoking a blunt is a new school way to describe it. The old school way was "he is hooked on those reefers" and "he'll be using Heroin next." That fate never happened to me because I was afraid of needles, and

I was coming to my senses by telling myself I was wasting my time and life happens every day and death only happens once.

Yes, I began settling down, and many of my childhood friends started moving away or going in other directions. Some of the common occurrences with my friends included getting married, going to prison, and simply moving onto a college campus or another city with their parents. I began going to nightclubs and private parties and found my way back to socializing again. I met a new set of friends who had things in common with me, and working and making an effort to return to school became a priority, not just what my elders wanted. Setting goals and getting ahead in life were for my benefit and no one else's and that was the real difference.

All of a sudden, I found myself working, going to school, and, as always, listening to music. The radio was always on when I was in my car, but playing it at home after a busy day of work was not always to my liking. I needed to go to a nightclub or a dance hall and listen to a DJ play songs. I would make myself ask the DJs for the names of songs, and I would often be the first person on the dance floor. This went on for several years, and I was invited to participate in an all Corvette wedding, and that is where I met my wife, Betty.

We talked off and on for many months, and I took her out occasionally, and we enjoyed each other's company quite a bit. I told her many times that she was one of many that I was courting, and I felt conceited and correct at the same time. She enjoyed music, and I met her family, and that bond with all of them continued until we decided it was a much harder world when we were not in each other's company. We had our ups and downs, and as it happens with many couples, our ups far outnumbered our downs, and we decided to get married, and we did.

My joke-telling and outgoing personality were some of the outstanding features that she enjoyed, and she was my opposite: quiet, often introverted, and, to my surprise, fun and loving. We and our families hit it off well, and the only regret I had during our entire marriage was the advice I always give newlywed couples: "I tell their parents, their family members, their friends, and coworkers to enjoy their wedding, enjoy the reception and always give your support to the bride and groom." However, "stay out of their marriage." That unwritten theory haunted us, but our friendship and our love lasted for 36 years.

It was Betty's encouragement and insight that saw the light of the entertainer in me. We hosted a Christmas holiday party for her coworkers at our newly purchased house in 1989 on a Saturday in December, and many of her coworkers attended. I played music for them, and we had a great time. I danced and took song requests and was my usual self as the life of the party. Then, one of the doctors came over to me. He said, "Rick, you play some really nice music, and you should consider being a DJ." I ignored what he said, smiled, and thanked him for the compliment, but his words stuck in my mind.

I went to work that following Monday, and one of my customers called me. During our business conversation, she said,

"My family is having a reunion in Detroit this weekend, and we are looking for a DJ. Do you know one?" I'm still puzzled about where the words came from, but the words "I'm a DJ" were spoken out of my mouth. She said she would get back to me and let me know if they found someone else or if they would use my DJ services. After our conversation, I asked myself, "What the hell did you just get yourself into?" I went about my day, and it was exactly 4:45 PM. Just before I normally went home at 5:00 PM, she (Val) called me to say I had been hired.

She gave me the times and the location, and I was pleased to hear back from her, but I was also terrified at the fact that I'd never done DJ work, and even worse, I didn't have a sound system. I had many new and old songs on CDs, a new CD player, and a dual cassette player, but nothing to connect it to and no one to help me. I then remembered that my golf buddy "Lonnie" was a sound contractor and perhaps he had a sound system he would let me borrow or rent from him that weekend. I contacted him, and he asked one of his technicians (Dave) to call me, and they had a Professional Audio Demo sound system available, and I jumped at the chance to borrow it.

When I arrived at his shop, he showed me the system consisting of two loudspeakers, a commercial amplifier, and a multi-channeled audio mixer. He also assembled it and showed me how to make all the connections without damaging it and how to position the speakers on the stands he provided for the best results. It took a few times to show me before I was confident enough to assemble it myself, and I loaded it into my car and took it home. I arrived home, took the system into my living room, assembled it again, and my wife Betty almost went crazy. She could not understand why I had to set that damn thing up in her living room.

I politely and quietly explained to her that I wanted to make sure I could assemble it without a problem that coming weekend in front of an audience. I didn't tell her how nervous I was about taking on a party in front of a live audience. She finally understood and allowed it to stay there for a few days until I loaded it into my car and took it to the dance hall that weekend. I went inside the building and managed to find a luggage cart and I loaded my equipment on it and proceeded to the banquet room.

The hotel had an eight-foot table ready for me and a black and white tablecloth they provided for the family. I put my equipment on the table, connected the wires as instructed, and used a low-cost, low-grade, drugstore-bought microphone as my announcement tool. A few days before, I purchased several CDs with new songs, and I bought a stack of CDs and Cassette tapes from home. I was nervous as a man standing on top of a building with the wind blowing. After I hooked everything up, I went on stage, stood in front of the equipment, and hit the power buttons. Everything turned on and was in working order.

I breathed a sigh of relief, picked up the microphone, and said, "Testing, testing, testing, mic check, testing, testing." I heard every word I said plainly, and one of the hotel staff members gave me a thumbs up to let me know it sounded alright. I stood on stage momentarily, looked over my setup, and said to myself, "Wow, this feels comfortable. I felt like being in the DJ booth and entertaining a crowd is where I belonged." It was a feeling I had never experienced before, and it was second only to the feeling I got when I said, "I do" to my wife, and we walked down the aisle as man and wife.

I was on stage where I knew I belonged, and that feeling remains with me today, and I will never forget it. I welcomed the family reunion members into the dance hall, and the person who hired me, Val came into the room. I was so glad that I had most, if not all, of the songs they requested, and we had fun.

After that I was blessed that many people who attended that celebration were event coordinators and friends who hosted events. My phone started ringing, and many of the callers requested my DJ services. I got on the phone that Monday morning and asked my buddy and his technician if the system they let me borrow was for sale. They said it could be, and of course, I was excited when I asked him, "How much?"

He responded with a reasonable price, and I made arrangements to pay. I kept my promise to pay the amount requested in a timely fashion because I knew I would have to use his company again for more equipment in the future. That was one of the first moments outside of purchasing a car or my house when someone trusted me with only my word as collateral. It was the most important life-changing decision that improved my life, and I am so grateful.

Yes, I think the modern-day credit score system is not designed to help the individual who needs help. The Credit Scores are what I consider the "Modern day economic Jim Crow" and are just another reason to deny you financial help or to charge you a higher interest rate to benefit the lending institutions.

I threw that in for good measure because I believe the system of "I give you my word" was much more helpful than the credit score system that hampers the financial well-being of many black and brown communities. Many deadbeat loans needed to be collected, and the institutions were forced to take losses, but how many losses and opportunities are lost because of the credit score system?

That is an unanswered question that will never be known until the credit score system is dismantled, and a sensible credit system is returned to benefit the communities that the financial institutions are meant to serve. I wrote this poem in another moment of frustration with my money situation.

I Just Don't Have It
by Rick Love
Wednesday, October 14, 2009

Money problems are always on my mind.
The need for more money happens all the damn time.
I usually spend more than I earn
and I try not to make a mistake.

I spend much more money than I make.
The need for more money seems to never end.
The bills grow higher as each day begins.
What happens when I don't have enough to pay?
Plus my resources are cut off and delayed another day.

I try to catch up my bills and it doesn't always work.
Then they added more charges that decreased my net worth.
Interest on top of interest along with a late charge?
What did I sign that makes my life so hard?
Did I know I could not pay it when I signed that bottom line?
Was I that impulsive when I purchased what was on my mind?

I just don't have it is what I should have said.
No money down in large print got stuck in my head.
In confusing small print almost illegible and shallow,
It said, "Easy payment terms and no interest will follow."

I was fooled that day and I spent too much somehow.
A dollar down and a dollar later and later was always now.
Earned interest from predatory lenders are not shared.
They left me broke, worried, and financially impaired.

What if I broke the law to get the money I needed?
If I never got caught, I would not have to claim it.
Am I not guilty with a plea bargain under legal advisement?
What is really best for me if I tried not to hide it?

I finally realized I couldn't afford myself anyway.
The truth does hurt and it goes without saying.
Being a responsible adult is a game that won't stop playing.
Interest rates and late charges are all worth complaining.
The politicians will have to do a great deal of explaining.
My difficulties are legal and they are manmade problems.

Who in this world will take the time to help me to solve them?
When I get behind on my bills, no one helps me one bit.
I'd better seek a bailout or just simply admit,
"Damn, I just don't have it…"

CHAPTER TWELVE

BOOKING A GIG

Making and confirming dates is the most challenging thing I do. Most of about 90% of all events I am asked to host are booked smoothly and without a problem. Asking for a deposit to hold an event on my calendar is usually fine. However, I've run into people who don't want to commit with a deposit, yet they don't want me to give their event date away to anyone else.

Some of those clients are good friends or family members who don't feel the need to secure an event with a down payment. Furthermore, I save an event that was booked several months before, and at the last minute, it is canceled or moved to another date, and the DJ is usually the last person who knows about a cancelation.

Add to that, the mistakes that are made by me and my clients about the times of the event and the day it is scheduled to take place. I've had clients tell me a date intended for a Saturday or a Sunday, and they give me a date that falls during the work week.

I mentioned this because it is a great idea to ensure the event's day, date, year, and times are clearly understood and written before accepting a deposit or signing a performance contract.

Yes, I've made several mistakes caused by lost data in my computer, not taking the time to write down the event I agreed to host, and double booking an event the day I thought the previous one was canceled. Being human is difficult when you let someone down because you forgot to confirm your agreement. All that is left at that point is an apology and, hopefully, forgiveness. Unless you are a law enforcement officer, clients are always right and must always be treated with patience and respect. As John Wayne once said, "Life is tough, and it's even tougher when you are stupid."

CHAPTER THIRTEEN

THE IDEAL SETUP

I recall many experiences setting up audio and, at times, visual equipment to host an event. The ideal situation I've experienced at most events is as follows: The Caterers get the kitchen. The Decorators get the tables, and the DJs get the dance floor. That, to me, is the ideal setup. I've been in many venues, and that ideal situation is not always possible. It is best to be heard and not overheard. Being in the center of an event gives the DJ the best scenario for centralizing the sound system and making his or her audio system easily heard and never overheard by everyone in attendance.

This sometimes means that setting up in an area made to be a DJ Booth is a good place to set up because of the floor plan in that specific venue. Furthermore, having an ink pen and a pad of paper handy is so convenient to write down important things you might forget. Such as the honoree's name, the group sponsoring the event, the couple who just got married, or the couple celebrating an anniversary.

It is easy to remember a name when you don't have to, but sometimes, when the pressure of entertaining and being asked many related and unrelated questions creates a memory loss... BE SURE TO WRITE IT DOWN when those important names are first given to you. However, many events have printed brochures or flyers about the event and the honorees, and they are also a great source of important information...

CHAPTER FOURTEEN

THE CROWDS

It is common knowledge that all crowds are different; they consist of just a few people to two thousand people or more, and each one demands a different audio setup. I found that speakers mounted high or low on speaker stands are the most effective because the sound travels over everyone's head. Speakers on the floor are also good, and they must be more powerful than speakers on a stand simply because the sound goes through people. The low-range or Sub-Woofer Speakers are meant to fill a room and move a crowd. Plus, low-range speakers are often felt and not heard. Again, it depends on the location, the crowd, the atmosphere, and the occasion for which you are providing music and audio equipment.

I have been in front of many crowds, and they have been young and old, tame or wild, sober or drunk, and cooperative or hostile. As a DJ, I consider myself not only in charge of the entertainment but also an ambassador of responsible behavior whose intention is to make people enjoy themselves and not be a ruler but an approachable leader they can trust. It is my job to be the reasonable person in the room and someone who will respond responsibly in case of any emergency or unwanted situation.

I remember hosting one of my first cabarets when a guy dancing with who I hope was his date jumped on top of her while she laid on her back on the dance floor. He humped and grinded as he pretended to have sex with her. The security guard broke it up and signaled me to cut the music off. I hoped he didn't end the event and peacefully got them off the dance floor and out of the building. I looked at the crowd after he signaled me to resume playing music and I said, "I guess I won't play that song again," and everyone laughed.

I also recall a wedding reception where the bride went topless for about 30 minutes! The groom grabbed the mic and said, "Fellas, this is the last time you will see this," I guessed she was a stripper before getting married. Then everyone looked at me, and the next thing that came out of my speakers was "You Know You Make Me Want to Shout" by the Dynatones. The crowd enjoyed my humor, and I realized there was a song to fit every situation. I am glad I listened to so much music growing up.

I hosted another wedding reception when the mother of the groom had words with someone in the bride's family, and their words turned into an altercation. The management called the police, and I walked over to the people who were involved and told them to leave right away and return in about 60 minutes. I was so glad they listened to me because four white police officers showed up in 10 minutes, and they looked like they wanted to arrest anyone at the all Black social event. They talked to me, and I told them that the people with the issues went home and that there was no longer a need for law enforcement.

They left without an arrest, and soon afterward, the people involved returned to the dance hall. They apologized to each other, toasted, and danced together soon afterward. I had no idea that things would work out that well, and I was glad about it.

Finally, I hosted a wedding reception that started about two hours after it was scheduled. The wedding party was in a limousine, and they drove around town for about two hours after taking pictures before arriving at the dance hall.

They had what was described as "only Champaign," and it was obvious that all of them were super high. The groom was so drunk they had to bring him into the dance hall in a wheelchair. Plus, to everyone's surprise, he threw up in the middle of the dancefloor right after coming in. It was embarrassing, and the dance hall staff was gracious enough to clean it up immediately. The wedding party took the groom to the bathroom to clean and possibly sober him up.

Whatever they did didn't help much, and he stayed seated and almost incoherent the rest of the evening. He sat down at the head table and never ate dinner and looked sick and nearly paralyzed. It was embarrassing as they had to skip their first dance, the Mom-Son dance, the garter removal, and the garter toss. The bride did the bouquet toss, and I filled in a lot of the empty spaces when I started the dance music earlier than anticipated. Plus, and even more importantly, I never made fun of or talked down to the bride or groom, and I made everyone comfortable that the groom was excited and celebrated more than he realized. He was so happy with his new bride, and I am sure they will be alright. The crowd appreciated my words, and things went along almost as they planned, and we had fun.

CHAPTER FIFTEEN

GIVE CREDIT AT ALL TIMES

It is important to give credit and praise to everyone, even if it's not due. Everyone loves praise as opposed to criticism, and always be willing to praise someone for what you might consider a minor thing. I always praise the clothes they wear, their hairstyle, their speech, their singing, and most of all their relationship, if any, to the honoree or the bride and groom.

It is never acceptable to criticize anyone over a microphone, and that is one of the most important jobs of a DJ. This point is covered in the next chapter and is extremely important to remember. A Microphone is an instrument of communication; anything said using it is a one-way street, and there are no rewind buttons to take back anything said. I suggest you be careful with your words and seriously read Chapter Sixteen...

CHAPTER SIXTEEN

THE MICROPHONE

It is common knowledge that the use of a microphone amplifies the words of the person speaking or the sound of anything that is heard. The microphone is a valuable tool that became available in the early 1900s. The technology has undoubtedly been updated and improved countless times and will never stop improving. It has hundreds if not thousands of applications, and the primary purpose of a microphone is to be heard and communicate ideas, give directions, provide entertainment, or make important or not-so-important announcements.

The rules of public speaking are "Stand Up, Speak Up, and Shut Up," and you must know when to do all three. Then there are people who say something and others who have nothing to say. This situation often presents a DJ's worst nightmare, "the Mic Hog". This is a person who wants the microphone to speak about everything they see and every person they know at an event. They talk over whatever music or presentation is being played or presented, and in their minds, they positively contribute to the event's fun.

There are many ways to present things, and talking over the music throughout an event is dead wrong. I've been in an audience many times before I was a disc jockey, and a sign of professionalism and courtesy is to follow the rules "Stand up, Speak Up, and Shut Up" as you use the microphone only to make an announcement. That is the best advice I could give anyone; having something to say is important. I will acknowledge that once in a while someone is hired or asked to emcee an event, and they often have good things to say.

I am selfish when I entertain, and having one person at a time entertain a crowd works best for me. Plus, I am always willing to share the spotlight if needed. However, having nothing to say and simply making noise is not acceptable, and it only shows how much they don't know, and they risk destroying the fun for everyone at an event. I try to make an honoree smile by saying, "Honey, you are the sauce on my spaghetti, the meat in my sandwich, the cream in my coffee, and the beats of my heart." Plus, I would often say to the birthday girl, "Honey, you don't look a day over fabulous…" I wrote this poem to reflect the moods I am in when my microphones are used.

The Microphone
by Rick Love

Shout it out loud or quiet and soft.

The words we speak might scare people off.

I want to be heard when I give directions.

I want to make the right music selections.

I hold the mic close to me or slightly far away.

Mounted on a stand or held in my hand

I want to be heard with clarity for all to understand.

I'm careful with my words and I remember where I'm at.

Be careful with the comments about being young, old, or fat.

Being skinny will bring a few grins.

Cheerfully greeting a lifelong friend is a great way to begin.

I use the mic as a tool or to make jokes.

I often hope my words are carefully spoke.

Words spoken in a mic are powerful tools and more.

It was Barack Obama who started "Just drop it on the floor."

Wireless or with a cord you won't be ignored.

All eyes are upon you waiting to hear what you say,

I was so honored to be there on that God given day...

Speak up...

CHAPTER SEVENTEEN

SITUATIONAL MUSIC

In my mind, there is a song that fits every situation. It is important to know when to play something or how long it should be played. One of my favorite sayings to the Master of Ceremonies (MC) is, "If I am playing something and when I hear you speak into the microphone, I know to turn it down or off. When you speak, I am quiet." That is the fastest way we can communicate, and I try to match each situation or comment a speaker makes or sometimes about the clothes they are wearing with a snippet from a song.

This serves two purposes. It relaxes the speaker when needed (more often than not, it is required) and adds humor when the audience is surprised to hear a song that fits a situation.

I actually learned about timing my response by watching a lot of the Three Stooges. Yes, I watched the Three Stooges quite a bit when I came home from school, and I began to understand how timing is almost eighty percent of filling in spaces, and the other twenty percent is the song selection.

I've also hosted what I will say were CRYSTAL PARTIES, where they sold items made from crystal, and they needed a song to highlight products presented during a presentation. That is where my knowledge of music and the song lyrics was first tested. There are no set rules to engage a speaker or an audience; all I can suggest is to become audience-friendly and part of the crowd, not just the person who plays the music.

CHAPTER EIGHTEEN

THE DJ ALWAYS TAKES THE BLAME

In every celebration, birthday party, honoree banquet, wedding reception, or retirement party, all eyes are focused on the honoree or honorees first, and the disc jockey or whoever is entertaining is always second. This means that if the caterers are late or the food they serve is awful, the DJ is asked to fill in for their mistakes and give positive thoughts and valid excuses to the crowds.

That is the main reason why I chose not to consume alcohol or get high before, during, or after an event. Suppose a fire, a fight, or an unforeseen illness occurs. In that case, someone in the crowd must have a level head and take on the responsibility of crowd safety, and I think that person should be me.

There are event coordinators at events such as weddings and birthday parties, and they are the people who should also take on the responsibility of crowd control and a spokesperson or, I say, a go-to person when things are not going as planned. The best event coordinators are in the background and are never seen or heard from unless a vendor, such as the catering staff, the decorators, or the DJ is not performing as needed.

That is when the coordinators quietly ask those people to make the changes that are best suited or needed for the occasion. Those changes could be anything from the food being cold, salty, or even late, to the decorators not having the correct decorations or dangerous decorations on the tables that are not steady and will tip over and spill the contents or start a fire if candles are used. This is especially true if the event is outdoors or on a patio that allows the wind and unwanted elements like the hot sun, pouring rain, or uninvited bugs to invade the atmosphere of an event.

On the other hand, the DJ might be playing the wrong music to the wrong crowd, and the coordinator received countless complaints about his performance or the loud music volume. In her infinite wisdom, my mother told me, "Anything we don't want to hear is always too loud." Those types of complaints are standard in every situation, from young to old and old to young. When I spin music for a crowd, I often research their ages and, of course, the type of event they are hosting and always keep in mind that every crowd is different and things that work for one crowd may not work for another or the same faces in the crowd on different occasions.

I have to keep in mind that no one wants to hear the same thing each time they attend a celebration, and I try to be as unpredictable as possible. That only applies if the group or people you work for do not select a format for that day. There are countless numbers of formats that are requested. The favorites that I've experienced are old school, featuring the music from each decade. In the hustle dance events, they do the new and the old hustle dances, and a ballroom and stepper's set features what I call easy-listening to adult songs.

All of those are good formats, and they all have their place. Of course, there is the Hip Hop format that fits where it's needed. I hosted an event for a crowd in their 50s, 60s and 70s and it was billed as an old-school celebration. After about an hour of the music they requested, they asked for the latest Hip Hop songs that I would've never played for them otherwise. I hope they didn't see my mouth when my jaws dropped, and they began twerking and humping each other as they waved their hands in the air. I was shocked and continued to play the type of music they were dancing to and enjoying.

The most successful events I've hosted usually start with light jazz music followed by old songs that inspire the elders in the audience. From there, the hustle dances are favored along with the ballroom and step songs, and that is when the liquid courage (alcoholic containing drinks) begins to surface, and the behavior of the crowds becomes more and more focused on having as much fun as they can and here again the DJ is the center of their attention. Also, note that during the final hours at an event, the elders usually leave the building or have gotten a buzz from what they consumed. The music no longer matters as long as the DJ keeps the beat and pleases the crowd who remains there to party.

CHAPTER NINETEEN

THE STRANGEST THINGS HAPPENED

It is not uncommon for things to happen at an event that are not planned or thought of. I've been involved in witnessing people having health issues like a heart attack, an epileptic seizure, a mild stroke, or getting so drunk that they pass out. I've witnessed a parent coming to get a child who snuck out of the house and beat them in front of the audience. Until that moment, I never realized it would happen anywhere outside of an elementary classroom or at home.

I remember queuing up a few songs and letting them play so I could go to the restroom. There were several parents in there with belts beating their unruly children because they poured soap on the bathroom floor and covered it up by unrolling countless rolls of toilet paper.

I walked in, politely walked right back out to another restroom down the hall and allowed them to chastise their children without interfering with their actions.

I witnessed a person leaving a drink on the bar and going to the restroom. While he was gone, another person asked the bartender for a drink. Within a few minutes after the first person left his drink on the bar, the second guy momentarily turned his back on the bar and turned around and saw a drink. He picked it up thinking it was his, not knowing it belonged to the person who left it there a few minutes ago before going to the restroom.

The guy returning from the restroom got upset that the second guy had his drink, and he pulled out a gun! He started talking loud and rudely to the second guy, and the bartender called the police. The police arrived in less than three minutes. They got there so fast that the guys at the bar were still arguing. The police had guns drawn and told the first guy to put down his weapon. He did, and no one was harmed, and they handcuffed the guy with the gun and took him into custody.

The bartender asked me to announce that everything was alright, and he allowed the party to continue. That was a real-life example of why some people don't need a gun. That was a real display of incompetence and unreasonable behavior that often happens when people drink alcohol and carry a gun.

As I mentioned in Chapter 14, a fight broke out at a wedding reception when either the bride or the groom's family disrespected one of the married couple's parents, and they began to fight, and all hell broke loose. I immediately turned the music off and allowed the rest of the guests to break up the skirmish. I got on the microphone and said, "This is the suburbs, and the police are on the way. The people involved are advised to step out and leave for about an hour before returning to the dance hall. I'm saying this because if they come in and find out who was fighting, they will take someone in custody, which would cost you more than a few weeks' pay.

I was glad they listened to my advice, and in less than 10 minutes, the police showed up. I told them that it was a minor disagreement, no weapons were present, and the people involved all left the dance hall. The guest thanked me, and I was given a round of applause when the people who had a disagreement returned to the dance hall.

A few minutes after, everyone sat down, and the confusion ended. I took a chance and asked all the people on the groom's side to make some noise. They did, and right after that, I asked all the people on the bride's side to make some noise, and they screamed twice as loud as the first group. I played "We Are Family" by Sister Sledge, and everyone cheerfully sang along. It turned out to be a great celebration. The bride and groom were overjoyed that everyone calmed down, and I made their wedding reception a fun-filled, memorable occasion.

That was one of my most memorable moments, and a not-so-memorable moment happened at a birthday celebration when a few guests fought over "a girl in the audience." A few more guests joined in the brawl and the fights took place inside and outside the building. The person running the dance hall walked over to me and asked the hustle instructor, Sandy if he could use our microphone. She let him use it without hesitation, and he shouted at the top of his lungs, "EVERYBODY, GET THE FUCK OUT! THIS PARTY IS OVER!"

I, along with everyone in attendance, young and old, was stunned by his words, and I was glad I collected my fee ahead of the celebration because it would've been difficult to collect it otherwise.

Finally, I was blessed with my daughter Chanell in 1997, and as she was growing up. I was away from home quite a bit and did not spend as much time with her as I wanted. We would play games like "say the letters of that word on a billboard" or "If you give me the first letter of the name of the toy you wanted, I might buy it for you." That word game did not last very long...

I took her to an event where she met another girl about her age. I would tell my daughter that she was going to work with Daddy because I didn't have time to get a babysitter. She had to do as I asked, and there was no second-guessing my directions. Plus, I told her I would give her money for good behavior, and she liked that idea quite a bit. At any rate, she and her new friend ran around the dance hall, and since they didn't seem to bother anyone, no one, including me said anything to them as disciplinary directions.

They ran around backstage and low and behold, they tripped and pulled the power cord that was attached to my audio system out of the wall. Yes, that meant my music cut off, and the sudden silence shocked me and the audience. I went behind the curtain, and there my daughter was, standing beside the unplugged cord with a sad look, and her new friend had the same expression. I promptly plugged it back in, and she knew she'd messed up, and she said, "I am sorry, Dad, it was a mistake." I accepted her explanation, and I went back to work.

After that incident, I was inspired to sit down and write the following poem:

Daddy, Please Spend Some Time With Me
by Rick Love
Wednesday, December 24, 2008

Daddy, please spend some time with me because you are never at home.

When you work so much, I feel so alone.

Sometimes I hardly know you are there.

You were even gone when they braided my hair.

I stayed up late some nights waiting for you to come home.

I even saved you the last slice of pizza before it was all gone.

How much do you make and do you get paid by the hour?

How much will it cost me to control your earning power?

Is it thirty-five dollars an hour or a little bit more?

Is it less than that to excuse you from the ballroom floor?

Can I borrow twenty-five dollars to add to my ten?

Will you give it to me now before your work day begins?

I'll add it to my total to add them up again.

It's not an unreasonable request for me to be my best.

It's not even bad when I get this stress off my chest.

Can I please have twenty-five so I can make it add up?

I promise to put it all into my charity cup.

I want it for you, and I won't ask for more.

I saved my money so I could even the score.

I really need you to spend some time with me.

You make thirty-five dollars an hour and that's good as they say.

Can I suggest something else that will make both our days?

I know you might wonder and you may not share my point of view.

But the money I have is yours just to spend the day with you.

I paid your salary for an entire day so here at home is where you can stay.

I love you daddy and this is just a start.

My money, my time and my love comes straight from my heart.

Please spend time with me Daddy and I won't ask for a refund.

You will never have to cash it in or share it with anyone.

Stay home today because all I can say,

It will be worth its weight in gold each and every blessed day.

There is really nothing else that I can say and all I can do is continue to pray.

Your time is my love, and it is forever priceless…

CHAPTER TWENTY

THE BILL COLLECTOR

The primary purpose of getting a job and going to work is to make a living and to get paid. This is a complex subject to discuss because many people live to work instead of working to live. The real meaning of having a JOB is defined as "Justification of Bondage" or "Just Over Broke," and finally "Jumped Outta Bed…" I heard or read a few of those somewhere, and the others I made up. This is one of the most challenging things that drives most if not all, of our actions: "Getting Paid." I really enjoy playing music for people, and it has paid a few bills and opened many doors that would never have opened if I hadn't become a disc jockey.

However, it is not always about making money to me. I have done and will continue to work for free in our community. Money is not always needed to satisfy my need to make people happy, especially our young people. It is a blessing to become an adult, and it's more of a blessing to become an adult who gives to others.

Our talent is said to be "A gift from God." When we share our talents with others, it is known as "A gift to God." I heard the words in a song by legendary actor singer-songwriter Harry Belafonte that said, "It takes a whole lot of human feelings, I know from what I've seen. It takes a whole lot of human feeling to become a human being…" I wrote this poem right an honoree did not pay me after I hosted their birthday celebration.

Fees

by Rick Love

Tuesday, January 05, 2010

Let's break this down so we can understand.
Fees were created and issued by a mortal man.
They were invented to make too many people pay
For the countless mistakes they make every day.

Some oversights are filed when making a claim.
They are forget-me-nots that have the same bad names.
There are late fees for not paying on time.
There are admission fees after standing in a line.

There are fees to enter or be dealt into a game.
There are fees to pay if you want to change your name.
There are fees to get married and live happily ever after.
There are fees involved to file a bankruptcy chapter.

There are fees to set you free when you commit a crime.
There are payments on top of fees to justify serving your time.
There are fees to pay for services rendered.
They cost twice as much if their documents are surrendered!
There are fees to set us free from wherever we may be.
There are late fees accessed if we are not on time.
They charge you twice as much, and they called it a fine.
A business receives a check for their services provided.
The bank bounced that check and you were blindsided!

They charged the innocent again along with a handling fee!
They did nothing wrong other than try to help me.
I received a ticket for someone else's deeds and I was outdone!
I received it from the county and it was twice as wrong.

I was under the impression that I had a few rights.
They've taken fees to the limits and to extraordinary heights!
Please explain to me how all of this took place?
Was this a challenge or a game to obstruct the human race?

The almighty dollar rules as time has come to pass.
Stand up for your rights and always dare to ask.
Fees are a way to squeeze more money from the middle class.
The rich get richer, and the poor gets kicked in the ass.

Winners never quit and, losers never try,
and fees have made so many of us cry.
Please stop…
Humanity does help the world to prosper…

It is also something to be noted: "Mrs. Credit died, and she left two sons, Cash and Carry. That is a gentle way of saying that too often, the people in charge of paying the DJs wait until the last minute as a way they believe to control his or her actions. That is the wrong way to handle it. Many bands and singers demand payment before they perform, and if the payment waits until afterward, a tip is most often given or, once in a while, expected. For obvious reasons, please ask your coordinator or the person in charge of making payments to take care of that important task as soon as they can.

CHAPTER TWENTY-ONE

I MUST BE GETTING OLD

This might seem like a strange chapter, but as just about every fan of old-school music will say, "The music was much better back in the day." I often tell a story about why I think the music was better by simply saying, "It is all about the money." Old-school music was written and produced when music and record sales were a highly profitable business. We had to buy a record to own it; downloading and copying was impossible for most consumers.

The writers, producers, and musicians knew they would sell thousands of copies every day if they made some good-sounding music. There was a record store on just about every street corner, and it was the so-called "IN Thing" to have a record collection. Add to that the record players used phonographic needles that would wear out faster than we imagined and a stack of coins (preferably nickels or quarters) were stacked on the playing arms above the playing needle to make it play our records until we could get those few extra dollars to buy a new needle.

With the options of downloading and copying, there is less motivation to spend three months producing a good recording and not getting paid for it. That is the real reason that many albums or CDs are no longer made for listening. They are made to promote the number one way recording artists get paid nowadays, "concerts"... Plus the new school way of distributing music by internet downloading is also popular, but I am not aware of the success or the profits they produce. Finally, I know I am old school because they broke into my van and didn't take any of my CDs...

I wrote this poem after my car was broken into and my speaker and a few stands were taken. It happened in downtown Detroit, only one block from the police station. Add to that, the cameras on the side of the building were said to be "inoperable" the night they broke into my car. Why is it that cameras never work when something happens?

They Broke into My Car
by Rick Love
Friday, June 07, 2013

I went to work as always and everything was fine.
I arrived at the banquet hall right on time.
I asked security to let me park inside.
I wanted to unload my stuff and not feel like I had to hide.

I went inside to get the story of what they could do for me.
They told me to use valet or park my car a block away.
I explained how I needed to be close to my car.
If I need something out of it, I would have to walk too far.

I parked right next to the door near the front of the hotel.
I put coins into the meter to avoid a ticket as well.
I came outside once about two hours later.
Everything was fine and I put more money in the meter.

I went back inside to finish the party I started.
We had fun, and there was no doubt about it.
I packed up my things and I was helped out of the door.

When I opened the security gate, I shocked with horror.
My rear door was open and glass was on the ground.
Something was very wrong and I began to look around.

They stole several of my speakers and a crossover device.
Along with speaker stands and that was not nice.
They left my DJ lights on the floor
and my credit cards on the door.

I used my club on the steering wheel.
It was not locked as they didn't check if it was real.
I immediately called the police to report what happened.

They asked me so many questions
that were irrelevant to the problem.
I was told an officer wasn't available,
and I was far down on the list.
They told me to be patient,
and I was really pissed.

Whoever broke into my car was a real live jerk.
Plus, they should be quite upset
that the stuff they stole doesn't work...

Please enjoy them,
you F...ing assholes...

Add to that unfortunate event, I thought about buying a gun to protect myself and my equipment, but after giving it many hours of serious thought, I really don't own anything other than my life or the life of a loved one that is worth taking a human life to protect. I wrote this poem out of anger, and hopefully, it will save a life after you read it...

Guns

by Rick Love
Monday, March 28, 2016

Invented as a weapon of death to do great bodily harm,
It was created as an instrument of protection
and a reason to bear arms.
Our Second Amendment rights
were created in America's early years.
To protect us from British soldiers and lynch mob fears.

Suicides and mass shootings are not uncommon.
They occur too often nowadays and seem easily forgotten.
Getting a gun permit for protection appears to be the answer.
More often than not, it leads to a disaster.

America's NRA means "Not Reasonable At All".
They control congressional legislation
where their money stands tall.
"God, Guns, and Guts made America great"
is the excuse they use.
The end results are suicide, murder,
and horrific headline news.

Buy an assault weapon or a handgun gun is what they say.
They forget to mention when the owners get shot anyway.
Once in a great while, a gun reportedly saves a life.
The odds are one in ten million
in spite of deceitful media hype.

If we get rid of the guns,
tragic gun deaths will soon drop.
America will be great again
because the senseless killings will stop.

Guns are an epidemic
that creates genocide and mass incarceration.
America, please solve this problem right away
without further hesitation.

Remember "All lives really matter"...

CHAPTER TWENTY-TWO

BRING BACK THE DAYS

Being a child in the 1950s, 1960s, and 1970s, I enjoyed a wonderful experience because of the great music. There were very few gaps in the age groups who listened to the same thing. I was often told that if the music had to be turned off when an adult entered the room, it would not last. That is a fact that remains in place today.

Rap music that talks about criminal behavior, harming people, or degrading each other is meant to make money and has no other positive purposes. I say, "If eight out of 10 records produced with the Black community in mind have to be censored for language, we are in trouble."

Plus, the last time I checked, there were 13,342 words in the English language, and if the songwriters we admire and the artists we follow as role models can only find less than 20 words to use in their songs, we should not give them our hard-earned money. I say make them earn it by showing us and the world they can be more creative.

I listened to thousands of hours of Motown, Atlantic, Stax, Chess, Sony, Verse, Malaco, and ABC Records, and very few words of profanity were used in their music. That is what should happen again. I can only imagine what would happen if the young men and women who stood under the street lights used profanity.

The parents on the porch and the people who looked for talent in the music business would never have made such an impact on the world. The police officers who lived in the neighborhood would've been called, and the talent of those musicians would have never been discovered and enjoyed by the world. Music is the rhythm of life, and all things that move use a beat to express or achieve whatever they are doing. This book was originally intended to express how to be a Disc Jockey, and all I can do is ask you to read the following and probably the final chapter.

CHAPTER TWENTY-THREE

WHAT YOU WILL NEED AS A DJ

First of all, you need to enjoy entertaining. Stage fright is normal and is often cured with time. I once read the meaning of the word FEAR. It was written: "Forget Everything And Run" or "Face Everything and Rise." Those definitions are meant to be confidence builders and the "No Guts, No Glory" theory certainly applies. If we never try, we will never succeed because failure is a byproduct of trying and a lesson learned when trying to succeed.

You must have the ability to smile on every occasion and respect the needs of an audience. That means "never disrespect anyone because of their musical preference and be willing to play anything they request to make them happy." This pertains to using any player, from a cellphone to a highly sophisticated computer system. Music is something that most, if not all, people appreciate, and listing all your equipment needs is almost impossible.

There are many venues and situations where being a disc jockey is nothing more than entertaining a few family members or close friends and the only rules are; to be nice, be entertaining, be comfortable, and above all be a part of the audience and allow yourself to become someone they trust to allow them or at times make them have a great time...

CHAPTER TWENTY-FOUR

THE CONCLUSION

Thanks for spending time reading this book. I hope to fill in a few more blanks if I feel I left anything out in my next publication. It is normal for someone to see the same act over and over again to want to change or see someone else perform and that is alright. That is the main reason why it is important to always be willing to change your music selections to fit the crowds and not just your music sclections. As the old saying goes, "Blessed are the flexible because they won't get bent out of shape…"

Add to that, don't allow your feelings to be hurt when you have hosted an event for many years and the management at that company changes, or the event personnel decides to hire another disc jockey or a band to replace you. In her infinite wisdom, my mother told me, "If you fill a bucket with water and put your hand in it, and you take your hand out, and it fills in the water afterward, anyone can be replaced." Just do your best and always respect everyone's opinion and perception of your music selections.

Please stay safe, have as much fun as life offers, and above all, enjoy the rhythms of life known as the beats in your heart and the precious joy of listening to music...Also, remember to have fun, and no one will get out of this life alive...

I will add a saying that my wonderful, deceased father-in-law (nicknamed LJ) said, "Only one man walked on water, and everyone else has to swim" along with my mother who told me, "If they threw stones at Jesus, we don't have a chance of making everyone happy either..."

As I go through life with a smile and a song, nothing is better than never being wrong. Being misunderstood or taken the wrong way will always be corrected and will wait for another day...It was also elegantly said, "It is nice to be great but great to be nice." ENJOY...

The Love family, then and now.

www.ingramcontent.com/pod-product-compliance
Lightning Source LLC
Chambersburg PA
CBHW040234110526
44582CB00002B/53